Memories of
Romford

The publishers would like to thank the following companies for their

support in the production of this book

Main Sponsor

Mullis & Peake

The A.R.G.E.E. Instrument Co. Limited

Chauvin Pharmaceuticals Limited

Matchroom Sport Limited

Romford Stadium

First published in Great Britain by True North Books Limited
England HX5 9AE
01422 377977

ISBN 1 903204 40 2

Text, design and origination by True North Books Limited
Printed and bound by The Amadeus Press Limited

Memories of Romford

Contents

Introduction

Our world is changing so quickly that there seldom seems time to stop for a moment and check on the period through which we have lived. We are constantly looking forward to what lies ahead without considering that we have left behind. If we are not careful the lessons and the achievements of the past will become lost forever, consigned to some distant, dusty recess of our brains that can no longer be accessed. 'Memories of Romford' is a publication that will help unlock the key to the historically recent times through which our parents and we lived. Already many of us have forgotten or never fully experienced life as it was before the onset of ring roads, flyovers and underpasses. There really was an age, not too long ago, when the car did not reign supreme and when children played with home made toys without the need of computer chips with everything. We had food that tasted of something other than plastic, people went shopping in the market for fresh fruit instead of designer jeans and families sat round tables together to eat their evening meals. They listened to the radio, grouped in front of a crackling set that brought 'Dick Barton', 'ITMA' and Henry Hall's orchestra into the front room. Out on the streets rag and bone men called out for business, offering to exchange unwanted household scrap for pegs to be used on the washing line and donkey stones to enhance the appearance of the doorstep.

Within the pages of this book the reader will be able to return to those days when our monarchs were revered and our newsreels were full of British achievement. At the same time you will be able to see Romford once more as it was when livestock was driven directly along the market plain, people drank in pubs rather than theme bars and the youth of yesteryear spoke with one another instead of punching text keys on their mobile phones. 'Memories of Romford' contains a wealth of carefully chosen photographs that will vividly highlight the middle years of

Conservative Party supporters make their way through Romford Market in 1965.

the last century, each image being enhanced with thoughtful and stimulating captions that will make the reader remember and, perhaps, argue about life as it was when our market town lived up to its description. Nostalgia is something that we all have in abundance and here is an opportunity to give that emotion its head. Each page that you turn will provide a talking point for something that helps focus the memory or emphasises something that the reader recalls having been referred to by an older family member. There is something here for everyone in a book that helps preserve an image of a way of life that otherwise might be shrouded in a cloak of forgetfulness as we hurtle onwards into these early years of a new millennium. There is no going back, but it is important to remember where we have been. We have been through some great times, though some tragic moments have come our way as well. Both the joyous and the heartbreaking are featured within these pages because it is from the double edged sword of success and adversity that we can learn to build a happy future. However, this book does not seek to preach or to provide a serious historical backward look. It sets out to provide the reader with an opportunity to let loose the waves of nostalgia that we all love to feel from time to time. Each one of us has individual memories of Romford as it was or how we think it used to be and here is an opportunity for some self indulgence in recollecting the face of our town before so-called progress took a hand.

Like all of Britain's towns, Romford's history goes way back into a past the like of which we can hardly imagine. There is some evidence that the Romans were here, remains having been found around Collier Row and Harold Hill, and there was the settlement of Durolitum somewhere in the vicinity. However, the first official recording of Romford did not take place until 1154. As the name implies, it developed as a settlement on a broad or 'roomy' crossing place over the river that became known as the Rom, growing in medieval times as a little market town on the main London to Colchester road. Little of the old water-

course is now visible centrally as, by 1936, it had been culverted within the town. The initial centre of population was probably around Oldchurch, but soon shifted to an area around the market place. So it remained for centuries, with only about 1,400 residents living there and along High Street, London Road and Woolford (nowadays North) Street in Tudor times though there were separate, smaller hamlets on the commons at Collier Row, Noak Hill

One of the floats taking part in Romford Carnival in the late 1960s.

and where Gidea Park can now be found. Romford existed as a sleepy place, only sparking into life on market days, though it had one moment of notoriety as the town was home for a while to Thomas Blood, the man who nearly made off with the Crown Jewels in 1671. Even by the beginning of the 19th century the population had only managed to grow to a modest 3,000, but Romford was preparing to make its own individual mark on the map. It had already become an important stop on the coaching route to London, but another form of transport was to wield its influence.

Several factors combined to enhance Romford's standing, but it was its early connection to the main railway line in 1839 that was of paramount importance. Within not much more than a decade land south of London Road, stretching down to the railway, was occupied by 200 cottages and a couple of factories. In addition, Laurie town, a development for the middle classes, was built to the east of the market and the population overall had doubled since the start of the century. Other developments followed, the most notable being on the manor of Stewards, on the east side of South Street, where 200 acres of land was built on by the National Freehold Land Society. Further building work in the later years of the Victorian era meant that the 20th century dawned with Romford's population standing at 14,000. Modern Romford really came to the forefront after World War I, losing its image as a rural town as new housing, businesses and city centre links with London turned it into a commuter suburb that began to lose some of its individual identity. The livestock market continued into the middle of the 20th century, but once that had gone and the Borough of Havering had arrived in 1965 the town lost some of its soul. 'Memories of Romford' will put back some of that which has been lost into the psyche of the reader, so prepare to pay a nostalgic visit to an era when Tiger Tim in 'Rainbow' was a child's regular reading material or when a holiday in Southend was more of a treat than a fortnight at Disneyworld has become. Taste the real ale flowing through the pipes at Romford Brewery and suck once more on a bull's eye or stick of liquorice root. Shed a tear for those lost to the doodlebugs, but rejoice to the strains of 'White Cliffs of Dover' as flags were waved and congas danced on VE Day. Count your tanners and weigh out your spuds in pounds and ounces because yesterday is just over the next page.

Street scenes

Looking along Market Place from the corner at South Street we are seeing the route of the old London to Colchester road, once a busy coaching run 200 years ago. In 1960 Romford was still a market town rather than a London suburb. In the distance a Morris Minor heads off towards Laurie Hall. It was one of the great successes of the British motor industry. Designed by Alec Issigonis, who also produced the top selling Mini, it remained in production from 1948 to 1971. A reliable car with excellent steering and cornering qualities, it was the first all-British car to pass the 1,000,000 mark in sales and surviving models are still cherished by owners and collectors. Coming the other way, the 174 bus to Dagenham took shoppers and workers alike to their homes or places of work in the Ford plant whilst the market continued in full swing as the focal point of the town's commercial activities. King Henry III granted Romford the right to hold a weekly market in the charter of 1247 with permission for an annual fair being given in 1250. It is from around this period in time that the growth of the town began along this section of what became the A118. Eventually, the market came to be held on three days a week, with Fridays and Saturdays given over to general trading with Wednesday usually acting as livestock day.

After El Alamein Churchill said that it was not the beginning of the end, but the end of the beginning. Some similar phrases could have been applied to what happened to the centre of Romford in the mid 1960s. The demolition men's ball swung like a pendulum, not keeping time but demonstrating that the times were a-changing, as Bob Dylan might have put it. The old market town was finished and the likes of Debenhams, C & A and others were on their way to change the ways of shopping around Market Place for evermore. Politically, things were on the move as well. In 1965 Romford joined with Hornchurch to become part of the London borough of Havering with a combined population of 250,000. The quartet on the pavement must have observed the scene with some trepidation for the work taking place was removing not just buildings but a way of life it had known since the early days of the 20th century. How ready was the man with bicycle clips around his trouser legs for ring roads and super highways? Could the housewife in her bootees turn her back on the corner shop, the market stall and the grocer or butcher as she entered a world of aisles, wire baskets and checkout tills in the supermarket? The chap with his hands firmly thrust into his pockets seemed to be displaying an air of glum resignation, but how would the fellow taking the rabbit back home for the pot cope with all this change? His was definitely a lifestyle that had no future, but one that had a past as rich as the gravy that would soon be covering little bunny.

Above: The usual picture of ladies who support the Conservative party is one of those wearing what are known as Tory hats and are normally gathered together at some garden féte. This group of mums wanted to give the lie to that image as they made their way through the market in 1965, the year in which Romford joined with Hornchurh under the banner of the new London borough of Havering. They slapped posters onto their children's prams to try to advertise that their view of politics had appeal for all ordinary folk, not just the cultured pearl necklace and twin set brigade. The aristocratic Alec Douglas-Home, after just 12 months as prime minister, had lost the 1964 general election to Labour, led by Harold Wilson, a man with a greater common touch. It was time for the rank and file Tories to hit back, so even nippers and toddlers were pressed into service. Their opponents responded in typical fashion, accusing these women of exploitation in using their offspring to play 'mind games', though such criticisms were usually levelled at the same time they were kissing potentially socialist babies! The building in the background was formerly St Edward's charity school, remodelled in 1930 as the first full time branch of Essex County Library. It closed when the new Central Library, designed by H Connelly at a cost of £180,000, opened on the old Laurie Square in 1965.

Top: This was one of the town's smallest pubs, situated on the corner of Mawney Lane and High Street. It was typical of the old style of drinking establishments where men who enjoyed a relaxing pint and a game of fives and threes at the domino table played traditional pub games. Other groups played crib or don, calling out to each other in terminology that modern youth probably thinks is a part of some form of pagan ritual. 'I've got Morgan's orchard and one for his nob to make five' could confuse even the brightest computer whiz-kid. 'Pegging the don and ten for game' would finish him off completely. The games still continue to be played in some pubs, but mainly by diehards and those of us with the occasional grey hair. Youngsters are missing out on traditional fun that is also more beneficial for them than poking away at a misspelled text message. The men who held the cards and rattled the bones at the tables could compute in mental arithmetic far quicker than it takes even to switch on a pocket calculator. Changing fads in drinking have separated the young from the old. At one time the Romford Arms sold Watney's Red Barrel, a keg bitter patronised by the youth of the 1960s who had key chains from which miniature red barrels dangled. Young drinkers now stand around and swig alcopops from bottles and seem to have made glasses and chairs redundant.

Above: At one time you could get more than your fill in the pubs that lay between the top of Market Place and Mawney Road. Even just stopping for a quick half in each one was something of a challenge for there were 15 in all. A market town like Romford always had more than its fair share of watering holes as large numbers of visitors on

market days wanted somewhere to wet their whistles. The King's Head was one of the most impressive, displaying an impressive frontage that had been a delight to both drinkers and admirers of architecture since 1898. The function room and hall inside was well used for dances, dinners, wedding receptions and musical shows. The pub's history went back much further than this building. The first King's Head was one of many such inns that appeared along the London to Birmingham coaching route. In the 17th century it boasted beds for 139 travellers and stabling for 400 horses, making it one of the most impressive stopovers for miles. Author Henry Mayhew described its back kitchen as being available for those travellers who could pay a little extra, but he also noted that it ensured a proper division of married and single men and women, though no one was so forward as to ask to see the 'marriage lines'. The inn was rebuilt in 1714, lasting for nearly two centuries before the next rebuild. The business moved to new premises within The Liberty in 1971.

The changing face of the town as it had developed in the 1970s becomes clearer in this view across Market Place. In the background we can see how the words 'high rise' have entered local vocabulary. On this day the market stalls had been swept aside to leave room for a small grandstand and spectator space as ice cream sellers did a good trade in keeping the crowd refreshed on a sunny day as road racers whizzed by on this leg of the Milk Race. Although the fine weather and the novelty of the occasion brought people out onto the streets, the ranks were sparse in comparison to those that might have turned out in France, where cycling is one of the major sports. Although nearly every single one of us has owned a bike at some time, it has never taken off as a huge spectator sport. In 1965 we voted Tommy Simpson, the first Briton to be world cycling champion, BBC sports personality of the year. He was to die in 1967 from heat exhaustion during a mountain stage of the Tour de France. The Milk Race, originally a competition largely for amateur riders, started as the Daily Express Tour of Britain in 1951, partly due to the efforts of Percy T Stallard who organised the first London to Holyhead race, which was the longest race in Europe at the time. His influence led to the setting up of the Tour of Britain and the Milk Race.

Unlike many other towns, trams were never really successful in Romford, so the bus heading off to the funfair at Battersea had the public transport sector on the roads to itself ever since the rapid expansion of this industry in the 1920s. Rail travel provided the only serious competition, offering workers at Dagenham an alternative means of getting to and from the Ford plant established there on reclaimed marshland in 1928 when the company moved its main production centre from Manchester. Other workers found employment nearer to home, making their way from the nearby railway station to the Romford Brewery that offered employment for 1,000 on its 20 acre site. This was a scene from the early 1970s, as can be determined from the short skirts, jeans,

platform heels, flared trousers and long, flowing hair of the young women, but they were not easy times for British industry. The voting public, tired of a Labour government that kow-towed to greedy, strike prone unions, booted Harold Wilson out of Downing Street in the 1970 election and installed Ted Heath's Tories instead. Things did not improve. Within a few weeks troops were put on standby as a national dock strike was called. More working days were lost to strikes in 1970 than in any year since the general strike of 1926. In 1971 postal workers withdrew their labour and Rolls-Royce went bust. By the end of 1972 a pay freeze was in force and the following year brought the three day week as power workers and miners took on the government. By March 1974 Labour was back in power.

Below: This blonde lovely did not actually get her hands dirty nor Tip Top Cleaners have any real hope of her custom drycleaning her coat. She was more used to parading along the catwalk or on the stage at beauty contests. The shovel of earth was part of a posed picture designed to attract photographers who love to see a pretty girl in their viewfinder. Good looks help to sell papers, as the Sun's page three will testify, and they also come in handy when promoting business. A girl draped across the bonnet of a car at a motor show does as much for sales as any talk of valves, cylinders and fuel injection. On this day it was the white coated manager of Leroy Furs who was hoping for a bit of extra publicity. The business was having some development work done and who better than Miss World to demonstrate the quality and attraction of the goods on offer. She would be pilloried by animal rights groups now, should she dress in real fur, but the crowd behind her was more interested in seeing a personality than in any political correctness. Autograph hunters, dressed in duffel coats with those awkward to fasten toggles, waited to pounce when she had finished her promotional stint. Her up to date 'kinky boots' offered a fashion contrast with the pin striped trousers of the man gazing at her in admiration.

Events & occasions

Excited crowds covered nearly every square inch of Market Place, cheering madly as the coach carrying the Lord Mayor of London arrived at the hub of Romford life in November 1937. One young lad, at the bottom of the frame, seemed less than impressed as he turned away and pushed his bicycle away from the scene. Perhaps that is unkind and he was merely attempting to seek out a better vantage point, though most little boys would not have appreciated the civic honour that was coming Romford's way. The town was about to be granted municipal borough status and Sir George Broadbridge had been given the task of presenting the charter that was received on Romford's behalf by

Charles Henry Allen, the former chairman of the urban district council and first mayor of the borough. The Lord Mayor's coach had driven past townspeople lining the streets all the way from Gallows Corner, along Main Road and into Market Place. Normally royalty would have undertaken the job, but this had been coronation year for George VI and he had many other engagements to fulfil as the newly crowned monarch. Some of them would help undo the ill will that his brother inspired the year before when, as Edward VII, he abdicated. Not averse to controversy, now as the Duke of Windsor, he was attracting shouts of 'Hail Edward' as he and his socialite wife visited Berlin and met the Nazi leader, Adolf Hitler.

Below: The mayor took the salute on the podium near the Cenotaph that had been erected in the 1920s to honour the brave souls who did not return from the Great War. The parade on its way to Raphael Park in 1947 included those who had fought so nobly in the second world war and as the crowds applauded them there was also the whispered wish that such demonstrations of loyalty and bravery could be consigned to the history books. The nation had suffered enough as successive generations lost the flower of their youth on distant battlefields. The regiment was passing the public gardens around Laurie Square, now home to the Central Library. These days the parade would have to access Main Road by marching across roundabouts and through subways, fighting its way through a concrete jungle. Laurie Square once boasted a number of attractive houses, including two particularly fine villas in the northeast corner that were demolished in order to make way for the library. It is ironic that you can now read about those buildings, but no longer enjoy looking at them. The northwest side of the square was bulldozed in 1968 to accommodate St Edward's Way. The roundabout at the junction with Main Road and Mercury Gardens includes a plaque that names it as Ludwigshafen Place, after the German town with which Romford has been twinned since 1973. This Rhineland city was heavily bombed during the war and citizens of both towns find the twinning a mixture of irony and reconciliation.

Right: Seen from Laurie Hall on Saturday 20 September 1947 from where the mayor watched, the parade carrying its regimental colours march past on its way from the drumhead service at Romford Stadium. It brought the traffic to a standstill and crowds lined the route all the way along London Road, High Street, Market Place, Main Road and into Raphael Park. The regiment had been granted the 'privilege, honour and distinction' of striding through the borough with fixed bayonets, flying colours and marching bands on all ceremonial occasions in recognition of its sterling service in defence of the realm. The chimney of Romford's brewery peeked above the skyline in the distance. Established in 1799, when Edward Ind bought the Star Inn and its associated brewery beside the River Rom in High Street, it was to become one of the town's main sources of employment. As a happy coincidence the railway station was built just 400 yards away, leaving ample space for expansion in that direction, making use of the transport facilities it offered. Brothers Octavius and George Coope joined forces with Ind in 1845 to form Ind Coope, one of the country's foremost brewers. By 1908 the brewery had extensive sidings linked directly with the railway. In the 1960s Ind Coope became one of the main players in forming Allied Breweries.

Below: The Bishop of Barking offered a warm welcome to the best loved member of the royal family we have had in the last century and more as she made a popular visit to the dioceses. The look of fond regard on the faces of the people standing behind her amply illustrates the level of affection with which young and old, rich and poor have always held for a woman who was to spend half of her life as a widow. Born Lady Elizabeth Angela Marguerite Bowes-Lyon, youngest daughter of the 14th Earl of Strathmore and Kinghorne

in 1900, she married Albert, Duke of York on 26 April 1923. At the time she was destined for a future life as a duchess who would flicker in the background of royal life. All that was to change when her husband was thrust into the limelight in the abdication crisis of late 1936. Within six months she was thrust from relative obscurity to being a powerful figure behind the throne ascended by her husband who had taken the title of King George VI. After a succession of foreign consorts the public was glad to welcome a home grown queen. Her insistence that the family stayed in Britain during the war instead of running off to Canada endeared her to a public who shared her grief when her husband died in 1952. Even in old age 'the Queen Mum' continued to appear in public, despite several operations for replacement hips and various skirmishes with fishbones. It was a national scandal that her centenary was given scant attention by the government in 2000.

Bottom: Photographed at Gallows Corner, close to where the flyover now marks the spot at a point where Main Road meets the busy A127 and A12, Queen Elizabeth II and Prince Philip were on their way to open the grammar school at Brentwood. Ever conscious of their appearance in public, the Queen wore gloves as a sign of modesty as much as to keep out the cold, as can be guessed from the travel rug that was keeping her legs warm. Her consort looked suitably dapper, neatly pressed handkerchief peeking from his breast pocket and an inch of white cuff showing at the wrist. Even though the drive past was taking place several miles out of town, in the late 1950s and early 1960s a royal visit was an occasion that demanded the streets being lined with Queen Elizabeth's loyal subjects, both young and old. Many clutched little union flags that they waved energetically as the royal fleet of limousines swished past. Some schools granted a half day holiday so that pupils could turn out in force, but that practice gradually subsided as most homes acquired televisions that meant families had almost everyday acquaintance with their monarch. Familiarity almost led to contempt, but that was the fault of the matrimonial antics of most of her children and not of our much cherished monarch.

This picture was taken c1960 when Princess Margaret, accompanied by the Lord Lieutenant of Essex, visited Oldchurch Hospital. The weather had been all too British and damp, so a special walkway had been laid and canopied to ensure that the royal visitor did not get her feet wet. The guard of honour included one person who was obviously making sure that she had her own personal memento of the day, snapping away furiously as the princess made her way between the ranks of nurses in their freshly starched uniforms. The hospital is built on the site of the old Victoria Hospital, opened in 1888 as a voluntary cottage hospital on land donated by William Mashiter. By

1937 it had been extended to accommodate 37 beds when it was taken over by Oldchurch Hospital, along with a neighbouring former workhouse, built in 1838 by Francis Edwards, that had since 1893 also included some medical facilities. Princess Margaret beamed a radiant smile on the day of her visit. She was enjoying a period of her troubled adult life that brought her great joy. In 1955, under family, church and political pressure, she backed out of an intended marriage with the divorced Peter Townsend. But, in May 1960 she found marital happiness with Anthony Armstrong-Jones, a fashion photographer. Sadly, her joy was not to last and by 1978 they were divorced.

Left: The Phillips and Meadows families were united in holy matrimony in September 1958. Bride and groom posed for the conventional pictures that would form part of a wedding album brought out on special occasions that would bring a warm smile of fond remembrance to the happy couple in years to come. Weddings at St Edward's often included a special mode of transport for newlyweds. These ranged from the carriage and pair used here to swish limousines, fire engines, brewery drays and steam traction engines, dependent upon the background and interests of the couple taking centre stage. As well as wedding guests, shoppers used to mingle with the crowd to catch a glimpse of the blushing bride and offer their own oohs and aahs as she swept into the church ready to tie the knot with her handsome beau. Since Market Place became marooned by the ban on traffic and the enclosure caused by the ring road such scenes have now entered the realms of folklore. How sad it is that the greatest day in a couple's life can no longer be celebrated in such a one off special manner. Progress may have brought us a smoother and swifter style of living, but it has also removed some of the delightful traditions that gave an extra sparkle and magic to days that should be given that little bit extra to make them perfect.

Above: Raise left eyebrow, lower right eyebrow and that is the Roger Moore style of acting, or so he would have you believe. The debonair heartthrob had a lot more going for him than that, even if he was never destined to grace the Oscar ceremonies. He could still laugh all the way to the bank after a career in movies and TV shows that spanned five decades. A Londoner, born in 1927, Moore appeared on the small screen in 'The Alaskans', 'Ivanhoe' and 'Maverick' in the late 1950s, in addition to a number of Hollywood film parts that kept him in the public eye. In the 1960s he became something of an idol in 'The Saint' and 'The Persuaders' and here is wowing two young fans in a promotional tour that brought him to the Odeon Cinema not long before he embarked on an immensely successful stint as 007 James Bond in seven films that broke many box office records across the country. His suave and urbane manner caused many a heart to flutter as he brought a humour to a part that Sean Connery had filled so well in earlier years. After his stint as the Ian Fleming inspired secret agent Roger returned to the general world of movies. In recent years he has dedicated a lot of his time as a good will ambassador for UNICEF.

Bottom: Oldchurch nurses gave a ride to a man whom was to become one of the most eccentric and mildly amusing figures of modern political history. Little was known of him in the early 1960s, as can be seen from the bemused faces of shoppers and traders in Market Place. But, for the next 35 years no general election would have been complete without his involvement. David Edward Sutch, born 10 November 1940, was an unsuccessful pop singer performing under the name of Screaming Lord Sutch, a name he later adopted officially by deed poll. Despite being a protégé of pop guru Joe Meek, his brief assault on the hit parade with such forgettable ditties as 'Jack the Ripper' and 'Dracula's Daughter' ended in abject failure. Determined to gain publicity for his stalled career Sutch turned to political stunts. He stood in a by-election created by the resignation of disgraced War Minister, John Profumo, as a member of the self formed National Teenage Party. He only polled 208 votes, but two of his manifesto items, votes at 18 and free dog licences, were later adopted. The publicity he got inspired him to continue fighting parliamentary elections, losing his deposit on over 40 occasions. He became best known for launching the Monster Raving Loony Party, a source of fun that actually got one of its members elected to a local council in Cornwall. Sutch could then rightly claim to be the longest serving party leader in the country. Sadly, in later years he suffered from manic depression and committed suicide on 16 June 1999.

Right: Norman Chisman was in charge of public relations for Romford in the late 1960s so he was well used to dealing with the people. However, even the best of communicators can look a little stiff and gauche when a gorgeous girl takes his arm in public. Her completely natural lack of affectation contrasted with the slight embarrassment from which Norman seems to be suffering, but most of the men in the crowd would have given their eye-teeth to swap places with him. This must have been one of the best perks of the job, for it is not every day that you get the chance to squire Miss Gamages and Miss Town Centre, all rolled into one, on a walk around Romford. Gamages, a branch of the famous London store that, each December, boasted the best Santa's grotto for miles, was one of the many businesses that opened new outlets as the face of central Romford began to change from market town into retail centre. In the background the cranes and derricks were busying away, shaping the new buildings that began to rise above and instead of the old ones. Fashions were changing as hemlines became more like pelmets, thanks to Mary Quant and her miniskirts. Soon many men would dispense with the old short back and sides as their collars and ears disappeared under lengthening locks. Barbers were out and unisex stylists were in.

Top right: Sir Walter Raleigh could not have laid his cloak any more graciously as did this page boy with his piece of carpet ensuring that one of Romford's best known characters kept her feet dry. All dolled up in her fancy dress she was off to yet another charity function to which she gave so much of her time. Nellie Sims started her working life as a

flower girl as a 1930s version of My Fair Lady's Eliza Dolittle. There was such camaraderie amongst the traders that, on a bad day, takings were pooled to help out someone who had suffered from a lack of business. Her market pitch, where she sold mainly English flowers, cost a shilling to rent, but by 1936 she and husband Harry opened a shop in the new Quadrant Arcade. These premises cost £5 per week, a large sum in those days, and the wartime years that followed did not help the Sims' business one little bit. Land was given over to the growing of food in the dig for victory campaign and little could be spared to help the lot of a florist. Nellie persevered and, with a mixture of hard work and cheerful personality, took the business from strength to strength in peacetime. Despite having her hands full with seven children, Nellie devoted some of her energies to helping others. Her charity work, especially for the cancer unit at Oldchurch Hospital, St Francis' Hospice and the PDSA, earned her the British Empire Medal. At Christmas time she dressed up and visited hospitals, cheering everyone up. She is seen here c1960 near her nursery gardens on Junction Road.

Below: It was rather naughty of the bus to be advertising the alcoholic delights of Haig whisky as it waited for the Salvation Army band to continue its parade down High Street towards its new Citadel in 1967. The 'Sally Army', as we all affectionately know it, despises the affect demon drink has had upon family stability. Unlike the Haig message, Salvationists have never been vague about their condemnation of all forms of booze. They came to Romford, referred to by their leaders as a 'brewery blighted town', in 1881. Not surprisingly, given the locals' enjoyment of a tipple and the jobs created by Romford Brewery the message coming from the 'blood and fire' brigade received a hostile reception. Undeterred, the first headquarters were established on North Street in the old Congregationalist chapel. In 1887 premises were obtained at the Wesleyan chapel on High Street and this remained

the central HQ until the new Citadel was built further east along the same road. Other halls were established in Collier Row Road and Chase Cross Road. Another opened in 1963 in Oxford Road. As the bandsmen marched off to their first service in the new High Street Citadel they might have reflected on how attitudes had changed over the years. Once they were the subject of vilification, but were now accepted as part and parcel of traditional British life.

Bottom: The Duchess of Kent presided at the opening of the hospital's new maternity wing. Clutching the posy with which she had been presented, this well loved royal took time out to chat with a group of overseas nurses. Their presence within the National Health Service has been vital to its continuation because nursing has been a poorly paid profession that has always struggled to recruit sufficient personnel. Nurses from other parts of the Commonwealth have helped shore it up, attracted by a mixture of dedication and better living conditions than in their homelands. Nearby was a set of old wards, from which some children emerged, their faces pressed up above the surrounding fences. The Duchess noticed them and asked that a detour could be made to visit them. A quick tidy up was given, but could not hide the unattractive brown tiling of what had been the old workhouse. The Duchess has always been a good communicator and who can forget how she consoled a tearful Jana Novotna at Wimbledon when the Czech blew a seemingly impregnable lead in the 1997 final against Martina Hingis? Katharine Lucy Mary Worsley was born on 22 February 1933 and married Edward, Duke of Kent on 8 June 1961. An unaffected Yorkshire village girl at heart, Katharine never felt qualified for her new role as a Duchess, but it is that lack of arrogance that has made her special in our hearts.

Compassing the law

The law is a noble and honourable profession with its roots going back millennia. In ancient Rome every member of the ruling classes was expected to participate in the legal process, being taught the law from childhood and in adulthood being expected to not only appear in court as an advocate, but also to take turns in serving as a magistrate.

Roman law formed the foundation of the legal systems of most of Europe, with the exception of England. In England the ancient and separate traditions of the British were preserved by William the Conqueror following his successful invasion in 1066. In those early days the business of the courts was to discover local law and traditions and apply them - the records of such 'discoveries' would eventually form the basis of the English Common Law based on precedent, later heavily overlaid with Statute law promulgated by the Sovereign acting, at least since the days of William and Mary, through parliament.

With its ever increasing complexity over the centuries few lay persons could hope to understand all the nuances of the law and this made necessary the creation of specialists to help guide the non-specialist with any difficulties they might encounter with the law. In England the legal profession developed two kinds of legal advisers: the first barristers, who specialised not only in very specific aspects of the law but also in advocacy, presenting cases verbally in courts. Few people had direct experience of such specialist legal 'consultants' - but almost everyone had dealings with solicitors, the general practitioners of the legal profession who would deal with the

Above: Company founder Fred Mullis.
Right: Fred Mullis' nephew, Lewis George Peake, who joined the firm in 1919.

vast majority of clients' legal needs referring to barristers only when very specialist advice was needed. And every town contains its quota of well known solicitors, including Romford.

North, South, West and now East. Over the course of a century in business the law firm of Mullis and Peake has boxed the Romford compass occupying premises in every corner of the town.

Mullis & Peake is a well established and progressive firm with an excellent reputation. Its policy is to provide legal services of the highest quality to meet the particular requirements of its clients.

The firm's founder, Fred Mullis, came up to Essex from Devon at the beginning of the 20th century and first set himself up in business in 1902 above a cycle shop in North Street, Romford.

The date of 1902 as the year the practice started has been established from looking at old records held by the firm - an early Law Fire Insurance Company register for example for that year is in Fred Mullis' handwriting as is an ancient mortgage register. Someone who would eventually become a regular client, a Mr John Basil Poel, is believed to have been Fred Mullis' very first client.

The firm would eventually build up a wealth of knowledge and experience in the commercial and residential property markets, in commercial litigation, property development, company and commercial law, licensing matters and of course services to private clients. In the field of residential development it would come to handle both large and small projects car-

rying out the varied legal work from option to acquisition through to planning to final sale. The firm would also come to act for industrial and commercial companies when buying, leasing or selling property and have the expertise to negotiate with local authorities as well as prepare and conduct appeals to the highest levels.

Around 1910 Fred Mullis took into partnership a Mr Surridge and practised under the name of Surridge & Mullis - by this time the office was at Bank Chambers South Street (over Lush & Cook's the cleaners) and almost adjacent to Barclays' Bank, the firm's bankers ever since. A London office was opened at 88 Chancery Lane; Mr Surridge however left the firm for the USA in about 1913 and Fred Mullis continued on his own. The firm would stay at Bank Chambers until 1923.

During the 1920s Fred Mullis' reputation would grow; he was chairman of Romford Conservative Party; the

Over the course of a century in business Mullis & Peake have occupied premises in every corner of Romford

Below: *John Poulton, Alan Lewis and David Fackler judging the Havering Schools Story-writing competition 2000, of which Mullis & Peake are sponsors on an annual basis.*

President frequently calling at the office to arrange meetings at the Corn Exchange (later Woolworth's).

Before then however Lewis George Peake had joined the firm. Peake arrived in February 1919 after being demobbed from the army. This marked the official start of Mullis & Peake. George Peake was Fred Mullis' nephew and came from the firm of Kitson, Hutchings & Easterbrook, an old established Torquay firm. LG Peake would go on to build a high local reputation becoming a member of Romford Urban District Council in 1922. Clerk to the magistrates in 1927 - and eventually receive the OBE.

Over the years the firm would build up a reputation for the successful handling of litigation matters and use its expertise in this specialised area to give a high class professional service. The firm's experience would eventually cover a variety of civil cases including commercial disputes, professional negligence, insurance claims and employment law. Early experience would pay off in the far future when at the close of the 20th and the beginning of the 21st centuries litigation would become an expanding area; with the high costs involved and the large percentage of disputes settled out

of court the calibre of the acting solicitors would become vital to act as both the sword and shield of clients.

In March 1923 the firm moved along the road to 71 South Street where it would stay for the next ten years. The new office was purchased from Essex Education Committee for £1,500 but the firm also rented the top floor of 78 South Street from the Essex Weekly News. 71 South Street was eventually sold in 1933 to Halfords for around £3,300.

Frederick Lionel Mullis joined the firm in 1924; he was the founder's only son; he too had served in the army in the 1914-18 war and had been taken prisoner by the Germans in 1917 having been caught up in the great tank battle at Cambrai. He would stay with the firm for almost 40 years, retiring in 1962 and dying in 1971.

Despite its small beginnings it was becoming clear that the young firm was destined for great things. In the year ended 31 March 1928 the accounts show receipts totalling just over £250,000, a remarkable sum for the period.

The following year, 1929, Thomas Frederick Fletcher joined the firm as a junior, he later saw army service in 1939-45 as a Lieutenant Colonel at the War Office. He subsequently qualified and after the war became a partner in the firm before retiring in 1982, dying in 1987.

Fred Mullis who had retired in 1930 died in 1943. Lewis George Peake retired in 1956 and died the following year.

Hard on the retirement of Fred Mullis in December 1930 however Frederick James Gerrey, also from Kitson & Co in Torquay, joined the firm in 1931. He too would be a long serving partner retiring only in 1965 prior to his death in 1980

Two years later, in March 1933, the firm moved yet again, this time to 6, Western Road where it would stay for the next 40 years - although between 1966 and 1973 the firm would also lease the top floor of Kemsley's at 10 Western Road.

The Western Road offices were bought from JG Gerrard for just £850; an extension was later built by Baker, Hammond & Laver of Rainham at a cost of £1,500.

An office in Chadwell Heath was opened in 1935 at 1A High Road leased from Messrs Ashton & Sons. One of the firm's longest serving members of staff, Tom Sharpe, was office manager there from 1935 until the 1950s.

Above: *Presenting the prizes in the Havering Schools' Story-Writing competition.*

Peggy Peake, Mr Peake's daughter who qualified in 1937, joined the firm that same year and was placed in charge of the Chadwell Heath office from then on until she retired in 1978.

Peggy Peake was only the 33rd woman lawyer in the country and Cambridge's first female graduate. Chadwell Heath was an all female office which was unique in 1937. It was said that Peggy who was a formidable woman would not have any men in the office - presumably with the exception of Tom Sharpe.

During the war many staff served in the forces, two of them losing their lives: Eric Seaward for example, a navigator in the RAF, was killed in a bombing raid on the German secret weapons base at Peenemunde on the Baltic coast in 1944. Another member of staff, Douglas White a lieutenant in the Royal Navy, drowned when his Corvette was torpedoed in the North Atlantic when on convoy duty in June 1943.

In the years since the end of the war the firm has employed just four pensioners as odd job men to do the post and open up in the morning; one of them, a Mr Bradley, went on until he was 96 by which time he was officially Britain's oldest employee. To mark his eventual retirement Mullis & Peake sponsored a horse race at Lingfield park in his name and he presented the winner's trophy.

The firm has a remarkable record for keeping its staff: a perusal of its records for the first seven decades of its existence shows some exceptional examples of long service: Nellie Ramsay who began working for the firm in 1929 and would still be found on the premises as late as 1970 despite having officially retired in 1958. Nellie would eventually become Mrs Blunt, her husband, Bill Blunt, having served the firm even longer, having being employed from December 1919 until October 1970 beating his nearest rival Tom Sharpe, who had begun work in 1920 and retired in 1957, by 13 years. Bill Blunt often recalled his first Christmas in the office in 1919 and could remember roasting chestnuts at the fire in the 'office boys den'. Nor are these unique examples of long service; Laura Smith, another long serving staff member who left the firm in 1975, had begun working for Mullis & Peake in 1935. Astonishingly even today 80 per cent of the firm's staff have over 20 years service.

Supporting its staff has always been important to Mullis & Peake: Charles Beard was an early example of this developmental philosophy, being an articled clerk with the firm from 1937 until 1939; after war service he qualified and joined Tozer's solicitors of Newton Abbot, Devon until retiring in the late 1980s. Today the company is very keen on promoting from within, allowing one per cent of turnover to be spent on staff training.

Over the decades many faces have gone to be replaced by new ones. The founder's grandson Cedric Lionel Mullis

Above: *Keith Darvill MP (left) and David Fackler (centre) setting out on a sponsored bike ride in aid of the Charity for the Lady Mayor, Maisie Whitelock, with proceeds going to St Francis Hospice.*

qualified in 1956 and joined the firm in 1961. Cedric Mullis was destined to be the last of the Mullis family to be involved in the firm; he retired in 1991.

Back in the 1950s and 60s the Romford business and legal community would meet for lunch at the White Hart where a table was kept and whoever could make it would have lunch for five shillings.

The firm's interests in licensed premises has continued. Over the years the firm has gained considerable exper-tise in the growing area of licensing law and clubs. To meet the special requirements of all the firm's clients including large breweries, night club owners to restaura-teurs, caterers and banqueting hall proprietors, the firm has become fully proficient in meeting all their needs. That expertise extends to acting for members of sports clubs and their representative bodies as well as giving specialist legal advice on legislation relating to Betting and Gaming, representing clients whether applicants or objectors in proceedings before the Gaming Board, the licensing authorities and the courts.

Many of the faces that sat around the table at the White Hart in the 1950s and 60s will be long remembered.

Below: *Staff proudly display the Investors in People Award the firm received in 2000.*

Peter Spencer, for example, who qualified in 1947 after war service in the Far East; he joined the firm in 1965 and retired in 1979. Peter Spencer had been captured by the Japanese in the fall of Singapore. He did three work stints on the notorious Burma railway and was in line for a fourth turn but he was rejected because the Japanese had one man too many. He always said that he would not have survived a fourth period on the railway. Surprisingly on his return to England he had a medical at which the doctor could only find that his eyes were not quite up to scratch

Other faces too came and went: David Gerrey joined in 1965, the year he qualified, though he later left to become a barrister.

In 1973 the firm moved to Marshall's Chambers at 80A South Street. Marshall's Chambers were named after the builders Marshalls Park Ltd, for whom the firm had acted for many years. The connection between Mullis & Peake and Marshalls Park (Romford) Ltd was a close one; the firm had been formed as far back as 1924 on the initiative of Fred Mullis. Marshalls Park had been bought for approximately £17,000; later they bought the Elms estate on the eastern boundary of Marshalls for £1500 so extend-ing the whole estate from North Street to Pettits Lane. Fred Mullis was a director of Marshalls Park with Lionel Mullis as company secretary.

Romford residents. As one of the area's leading solicitors the firm has been involved in the lives of many local families who have come to rely on the firm to deal caringly and confidently with their personal affairs. Naturally part of the firm's work covers divorce and litigation, probate, trusts and making wills - all areas which need to be handled with discretion and sensitivity. And of course moving house: the firm maintains a large department dealing with all aspects of residential conveyancing. Not only does the firm rely upon years of traditional experience but also constantly updates, strengthens and increases its expertise in the field.

Company and commercial legal law would be a continuing theme with the practice. Mullis & Peake today act for both private and public companies, partnerships and individuals and other corporate bodies. The commercial sector is active with new start ups, mergers, flotations, joint ventures and management buy-outs as well as insolvencies and liquidations. Swift legal advice is invaluable to business; Mullis & Peake place great emphasis on giving a swift response to clients' needs and adopt a very flexible approach to solving problems large and small.

The move to new premises presaged an era of growth. In 1986 the firm of AW Armon-Jones Hornchurch was acquired. May 1988 saw an amalgamation with Sanders, Poulten & Co of Upminster, a firm which had been established since 1954. And in August 1991 A Martin & Co of Romford was also acquired.

But there would still be reminders of the firm's long history. The world is full of strange coincidences. Back in 1912 when the Titanic sank one of the survivors was Eva Hart; she would one day become one of the firm's clients - but who could have predicted that the pub opposite the firm's offices would be named after her?

In April 2001 Mullis & Peake moved finally to 8-10 Eastern Road, a 1970s office block occupied solely by the firm, thus completing their trip around the Romford compass which had begun so long ago in North Street. Although having had innumerable commercial and business clients it is however through the memories of individuals that Mullis & Peake lives on in the minds of

Founded by two west country men and run for many years by their descendants Mullis & Peake has evolved over ten decades into a very substantial practice. But the firm has always prided itself on remaining very much a local firm looking after all aspects of the town and every part of the buyer's business. Latterly the firm has had to become more specialised in commercial business with many blue chip clients. The present partners have solid local connections, are alive to the challenges and opportunities of today and are quick to provide the imagination, breadth of vision and wide ranging expertise required to provide a professional service with a personal approach to all its clients.

The story of the legal profession continues to evolve. Today the historic division between the work of barristers and solicitors is becoming ever more blurred with individual solicitors not only tending to become more specialised within larger partnerships but also extending their brief to appearances in court, taking over some of the roles traditionally occupied by barristers. Who can say where Mullis & Peake will go from here - but if the past is any guide to the future the firm can surely look forward with some confidence to another century of growth.

Top left: *The probate department (Cameron Emslie, left, and Fred Rew, right) presenting a cheque to St Francis Hospice. The money was raised during the national "Make a Will Week".*

It is only some time after the war that people came to realise the true extent of the German bombing raids on our towns and cities. Censorship was rife in an attempt to maintain morale and only neighbours and relatives of those directly affected by the various blitzes on our communities fully appreciated the death and destruction that came with the hail of fire that fell from the skies during those dismal and frightening years of the early 1940s. Even in those circumstances there was only limited knowledge of the widespread havoc that had been wrought upon both industry and residential areas. Many private citizens had cameras and photographs confiscated as the authorities sought a fine balance between keeping the population alert and panicking the masses. Equipment removed from local photographers was locked away in Chelmsford police station, but there were still many box Brownies that stayed in their owners' hands. The first bombs fell in the summer of 1940, following the evacuation at Dunkirk when we knew that the phoney war, that period since September 1939 when little affected us directly, had come to an end. It started in earnest and escalated dramatically so that, within a few months, we were all touched by the hostilities. None more so than those who had to seek the assistance of the armed forces and civil defence personnel in trying to sift through the wreckage of what had been the family home.

Wartime

Both pages: In 1939 Britain's Prime Minister Neville Chamberlain had made his announcement to the waiting people of Britain that '...this country is at war with Germany.' The country rolled up its sleeves and prepared for the inevitable. This war would be different from other wars. This time planes had the ability to fly further and carry a heavier load, and air raids were fully expected. Air raid shelters were obviously going to be needed, and shelters were built on open places across towns and cities.

By the time war was declared an army of volunteers of both sexes had already been recruited to form an Air Raid Protection service. At first ARP personnel were unpaid volunteers but when war broke out in September 1939 they became paid staff. It was their job to patrol specified areas, making sure that no chinks of light broke the blackout restrictions, checking the safety of local residents, being alert for gas attacks, air raids and unexploded bombs. The exceptional work done by Air Raid Wardens in dealing with incendiaries, giving first aid to the injured, helping to rescue victims from their bombed-out properties, clearing away rubble, and a thousand and one other tasks became legendary; during the second world war nearly as many private citizens were killed as troops - and many of them were the gallant ARP wardens.

At the beginning of the war Sir Anthony Eden, Secretary of

State for War, appealed in a radio broadcast for men between 17 and 65 to make up a new force, the Local Defence Volunteers, to guard vulnerable points from possible Nazi attack. Within a very short time the first men were putting their names down. At first the new force had to improvise; there were no weapons to spare and men had to rely on sticks, shotguns handed in by local people, and on sheer determination. Weapons and uniforms did not become available for several months.

In July the Local Defence Volunteers was renamed the Home Guard, and by the following year were a force to be reckoned with. Television programmes such as 'Dad's Army' have unfortunately associated the Home Guard with comedy, but in fact they performed much important work. The Guard posted sentries to watch for possible aircraft or parachute landings at likely spots such as disused aerodromes, golf courses on the outskirts of towns, local parks and racecourses. They manned anti-aircraft rocket guns, liaised with other units and with regular troops, set up communications and organised balloon barrages.

Other preparations were hastily made. Place names and other identifying marks were obliterated to confuse the enemy about exactly where they were. Notices went up every-where giving good advice to citizens on a number of issues. 'Keep Mum - she's not so dumb' warned people to take care what kind of information they passed on, as the person they were speaking to could be an enemy.

Older readers will remember how difficult it was to find certain items in the shops during the war; combs, soap, cosmetics, hairgrips, elastic, buttons, zips - all were virtually impossible to buy as factories that once produced these items had been turned over to war work. Stockings were in short supply, and resourceful women resorted to colouring their legs with gravy browning or with a mixture of sand and water. Beetroot juice was found to be a good substitute for lipstick. Clothes rationing was introduced in 1941, and everyone had 66 coupons per year. Eleven coupons would buy a dress, and sixteen were needed for a coat. The number of coupons was later reduced to 40 per person. People were required to save material where they could - ladies' hemlines went up considerably, and skirts were not allowed to have lots of pleats. Some found clever ways around the regulations by using materials that were not rationed. Blackout material could be embroidered and made into blouses or skirts, and dyed sugar sacks were turned into curtains.

All the hopes and dreams of families, the years of memories and treasured recollections, the sense of belonging and security disappeared in the blink of an eye. Perhaps bricks and mortar could be reassembled, but feelings and simple things like personal mementoes were lost forever. As well as the death and damage the bombs of World War II brought, there was that sense of invasion of privacy and helplessness that infected ordinary citizens like a canker that could not be scrubbed away. After the Battle of Britain had been fought and won by those brave young men flying their Spitfires and Hurricanes in the skies over Kent and neighbouring counties, Hitler, denied the opportunity to launch an invasion of our land, ordered Goering to unleash his Luftwaffe bombers on our industry and civilian population. Repeated bombing raids over the London docks meant that the sky appeared to play host to a permanent sunset. By 20 September 1940 Romford felt the backlash of German raids as bombs fell on Carlton Road, Havering Drive, Kingston Road, Main Road and Oaklands Avenue. The largest crater in Essex was that created by a parachute mine that blasted a space larger than Quatermass's pit between Carlton Road and Stanley Avenue. The terror raids continued throughout the winter, only easing off in early spring. It was relatively quiet for the following two years, but no one dared relax. Then came the doodlebugs and V2 rockets and the horrors came back to haunt us.

Most of us have never seen a doodlebug at close range and we can be thankful for that. This was the nickname given to the reprisal weapon, the vergeltungswaffe or V-1 flying bomb, that Hitler began launching from bases in Pas de Calais shortly after Allied troops invaded Normandy in the D-Day landings of June 1944. Also known as buzz bombs, they flew low across the Channel powered by petrol and compressed air. The whine of the engine noise was frightening, but it was the silence when the fuel ran out and cut the engine that signalled the true danger. Then the machine, packed with high explosive, plummeted to earth and caused mayhem wherever it crashed. Parts of Kent and Sussex became known as 'bomb alley' and local inhabitants breathed a guilty sigh of relief when they heard one overhead as they knew it was going to fall on someone further down the line. Romford was on the right or wrong side of the capital, dependent upon your viewpoint, and was comparatively lightly affected, though 21 people lost their lives to the doodlebugs. The National Fire Service exhibited this unexploded bomb in Market Place on 18 October 1944 in aid of their benevolent funds. Over 5,000 people came to look at the contraption, contributing £100 to the charity. The spherical shape on the lorry is not a cannonball but one of two wire bound objects that provided the power to operate the control surfaces and fuel injection.

Bird's eye view

I n this aerial view of Romford the reader will be able to pick out some of the places that are no longer with us or have been obscured by new road developments. South Street runs up from the bottom of the photograph, towards St Edward's Church on Market Place before crossing into North Street. Moving along South Street you can see the Ritz cinema that opened in 1938, becoming the ABC in 1962 and the Cannon in 1986. Then there is the old Congregational church, built in 1883 to replace the 1877 building that was soon lost in a fire. It was demolished in the 1970s. To the left the brewery site, the telephone exchange and Co-operative Hall can all be identified, whilst, next to the bowling green on the right, the Plaza cinema stands out. It opened on 20 January 1930, becoming the Gaumont in 1950 before closing its doors on 15 September 1962. The site is now part of The Liberty shopping complex. Further on, St Edward's still provides a firm link with the past. The original chapel was consecrated in 1410, whilst the present building, designed by John Johnson, dates from 1850, though two vestries were added in 1855. The buildings over towards the top right, laid out in rectangular fashion, belong to Romford Technical School.

Left: In 1960 traffic flowed through the centre of the town, though it can be seen that it was starting to build up towards the proportions that would eventually lead to the levels of congestion that led the authorities to rethink their whole approach to the motor car. Over to the left car parks were filled with vehicles that had brought shoppers to visit Market Place, in the centre of the photograph, a spot that was doing a roaring trade just as it had for centuries and continues still to do, though the style and content of the stalls may have changed. St Edward's Church, just above the junction with North Street and South Street, still dominates the scene today, though it has to do battle for recognition against the shopping malls and ring roads. The church of St Edward the Confessor followed several chapels that had formerly occupied the site, dating back to the early 15th century. The new church was built in 1850 to acknowledge the independence of Romford parish from that of Hornchurch, to which it had been tied until 1848. The pilot and cameraman taking this shot were in for an unpleasant surprise when they came in to land. An eagle eyed policeman, presumably one who had got out of bed on the wrong side that morning, reported the pair for flying too low over the town centre. Quite how he measured the height has been lost in the mists of time.

Above: This aerial view of the municipal borough was taken in 1948 at a time when we were beginning to wonder if we had really won the war or that hostilities had properly ceased. Rationing still bit hard, Mahatma Ghandi was assassinated, Jews and Arabs clashed in Jerusalem, the Russians blockaded Berlin, rubber planters were murdered in Malaya and America's witch hunt of communists via its Un-American Activities Committee went into action. Even Don Bradman, the world's finest ever batsman, bowed out of Test cricket with a duck and London's Olympic Games were dubbed the 'austerity games'. On the brighter side, of which there was not much, the National Health Service was born, Freddie Mills won boxing's world light heavyweight title and a first grandchild for King George VI and Queen Elizabeth came into the world. Christened Charles Phillip Arthur George, he did seem blessed with noticeable ears. In this photograph the railway line runs diagonally from left to right towards the goods yard and siding, passing over South Street and the roads to Hornchurch and Elm Park. Market Place and High Street run roughly parallel with the railway line across the lower centre, leading out towards the town hall and the leafy avenue of Main Road. Little of old Victorian Romford remained by this time and nowadays the arterial and ring roads around the town centre would dominate the aerial view.

At leisure

ycling became an even more popular pastime for young women during the late 1930s and after the war. The League of Health and Beauty encouraged them to take exercise, showing that it could be fashionable as well as beneficial fun. Girls had an excuse to don shorts that would have scandalised their grannies as they pedalled away down the road. The cyclist on the left showed as much leg as the girls posing on the carnival float, but her display was demure in comparison to the provocative pose struck by the winsome pair riding on the wings. The procession had come up Main Road as far as Blacks Bridge and was about to turn into Raphael Park where merrymaking would begin in earnest. Some of the floats had come from out of town and their owners were soon to discover first hand knowledge of the gaiety of Romford's celebrations. Lying to the northeast of the town, this area once formed part of the manor of Gidea Hall, from which Gidea Park takes its name. Simon of Gidiehulle and his daughter held the lands in the 13th century, with ownership passing to Sir John of Havering in the following century. A succession of wealthy merchants owned it in turn, including the influential Cooke family, leading local gentry of Tudor and Jacobean times. Eventually in the 1880s the estate was put on the market for development, but the deal stagnated until Sir Herbert H Raphael bought the house and 480 acres of land in 1897. In 1902 he donated 20 acres and the lake for public use and the park was named after him.

What a jolly day these tots had at carnival time. The sun shone and their mums glowed with pride as they prepared their little ones for the parade through the streets on the back of the lowloader that acted as their float for the day. Hair was washed, combed, plaited and bedecked with pretty ribbons. Dresses were carefully starched and ironed as even the plainest Jane became a little beauty and the apple of dad's eye. Who knows if any of Raye's Babes ever got to Broadway, but did anyone really care? The little girls in the troupe, of varying shapes and sizes, just loved to tap, pirouette and delight everyone who enjoyed their youthful innocence and exuberance. They squealed with delight when they won their little trophies at shows and competitions, though it is likely that their parents and teachers had even more pride in their achievements than the children did themselves. Somewhere at the back of a mantelpiece or gathering dust in a box in the attic you might find a small cup or medal that belonged to one of these youngsters. It may seem a tiny item, of little intrinsic value, but to someone out there it is a memento that evokes memories of happy days under a cloudless sky or cherished memories of carefully choreographed flying feet in a dance studio.

Left: Performing a good impression of Wishee-Washee or a member of George Formby's Chinese laundry, William Pike enjoyed one of the perks of the job in his mayoral year of 1960-61. He was allowed to let his hair down and be normal, rather than the stuffy persona he had to adopt in the council chamber. However, he kept his chain of office around his neck just in case you forgot who he was. Rickshaw rides for the children at two for a tanner were provided by the alderman, with some help from a youngster so well turned out in his little bow tie. That little chap leading the way will now be well into his 40s. Does he still go for a day out dressed in his best dicky bow, with hair neatly slicked and parted to the side. Would it be too rude to suggest that going out wearing any form of tie is now reserved for weddings and funerals or that his hair just might be thinning into an even wider parting than he had in 1960? The occasion was one of the many fund raising events associated with parent teacher and school associations that are part of the traditional way of life our schools have had as long as we can remember. Although primarily fund raising exercises, these events are also good fun as part of community life. The Round Table also took part in this fête held at the top of the market in aid of St Edward's School coffers. Mayor Pike took the children from below the Town Hall and across Laurie Square, but made the return journey at a more leisurely rate.

Below: Speedway dodgem style cars were part of the fun of the fair as Romford Carnival drew to a close. The carnival queen had enjoyed her day riding on the processional float and being crowned as the town's symbol of beauty and charm for the next 12 months. One of her first engagements was to hang on tight to her insignia of office as various macho males did their best to impress her with their driving and bumping skills. Budding Fangios tried hard to show the girls how skilful they were and dads introduced their lads to fun behind the wheel, even if their sons had to keep their schoolcaps firmly on their heads as they were chauffeured around the circuit. Elsewhere in the fair couples cuddled on board the ghost train, with passion often giving way to feigned terror as ghostly skeletons induced the girls into a bout of screaming that frustrated their boyfriends' attempts at whispering sweet nothings. The waltzers provided more thrills as the bucket shaped contraptions whirled from side to side, often having been given an extra spin by a darkly dangerous fairground worker. He was the sort our mothers had warned us about, but it cost nothing to look and we were more concerned about making sure that the goldfish we had won at hoop-la did not become airborne out of its little plastic bag as we were hurled this way and that.

Centre: No Christmas party in the 1950s would have been complete without silly games that were a chance for old and young alike to let their hair down. Even the most sedate of grannies threw her all into pass the parcel and musical chairs. This get together had inspired the guests to put on their best clothes, as was only right and proper, and one chap in the background graced the occasion by putting on evening dress and a smart bow tie. Centre stage was held by the woman who, despite her favourite party frock, made sure that she was warm and comfortable in her cardie and slippers. She demonstrated a neat flick of the hips in keeping the hula-hoop spinning around her waist. Like so many other supposedly children's toys, this fad of the late 1950s was commandeered by adults anxious to show that they still had something of the child in them. The gyrations needed to keep the hoop from falling to the floor were supposed to mimic the Hawaiian religious, fertility dance originally performed in front of kings. At other parties parents borrowed their youngsters' yo-yos and competed fiercely with one another, trying to persuade everyone that there was life in the old dog yet. When trying the limbo dance under a pole in the 1960s they realised that they had taken silliness one step too far, collapsing in an arthritic heap as befitted their status!

Right: The carnival float containing little Red Indians, or native Americans for the politically correct, was loaded with children having fun dressing up as a miniature Hiawatha or Minnie-ha-ha. Coming along South Street, as seen from the railway bridge, past Times furnishing, the building on the left will be remembered as the Havana, from 1949 the Odeon, Cinema. The 2,500 seater building was designed by Kemp and Tasker and included a Compton organ and attractive café. It also held shows, including 1960s grunt and grapple events when Mick McManus and Jackie Pallo wrestled one another, but is best remembered as the place where many a courting couple found some privacy on the back row. The first films to be shown by Victory Super Cinemas on 29 January 1936 were by way of a double feature, 'Passing of the third floor back' and 'Stranded'. Such a programme was common and cinemagoers also expected a cartoon and a newsreel thrown in for good measure. The main film starred Conrad Veidt and was about a Christ-like visitor to a boarding house who changes the life of the other inmates. The 'B' movie was a forgettable tale of a woman working for Traveller's Aid who meets an old school beau. The Odeon was split into a three cinema complex in 1974 and closed in 1990.

Bottom: Ring out the old and ring in the new. This pretty girl, showing a neat leg and a few inches of fashionable petticoat that would swirl out provocatively when she danced the jive, had been crowned as the symbol of the end of one decade and the start of another at the New Year celebrations. She sat at the cusp of two very different periods of history. Born a war baby she had entered the 1950s as a schoolgirl promised free education for all until the age of 15 in one of three types of secondary school, grammar, secondary modern or technical. Her younger siblings benefited from free orange juice and school milk as she worried about older relatives sent off to fight in Korea, Kenya or Cyprus. As she proudly clutched her cup she remembered the continued struggle her parents had with rationing that lasted until 1954 and saw the smile return to their faces when the austere times were finally left behind in the Macmillan 'never had it so good' years. Her taste in music was about to change. At this moment she enjoyed Emile Ford's 'What do you want to make those eyes at me for', a reworked oldie that was top of the pops at the end of 1959. By the end of the next decade she would have seen the Beatles have the first and last of their 17 chart toppers. The swinging 60s would bring her a Labour government once more, man walking on the moon, colour television and England winning soccer's World Cup.

Below: It was party time at the King's Head in a scene that brought back memories of wartime dances that were held there, especially as the orchestra was made up mainly of female musicians reminiscent of the great Ivy Benson

Band. Even after the war, as here, many women relived the moments of fun they or their mothers had that helped them through the dark days by dancing to old Glenn Miller favourites, but it was when such cheerful tunes as the 'Hokey Cokey' or 'Conga' were played that they really went to town. 'Knees up Mother Brown' was another favourite that encouraged normally sedate women to raise their skirts and go for the high kicking routine of the Tiller Girls, though most shied away from ending their performance with a demonstration of the splits. In these situa-tions women have always been less inhibited than men. Whether it is the dance hall or the disco, each decade has had its own ritually performed dance and daft steps or actions to accompany it. In the 1960s it was the 'Locomotion', the 1970s followed with 'YMCA', the 'Birdie Song' and 'Agadoo' graced the 1980s and the millennium came to a close with us still performing a sort of line dance to Whigfield's 'Saturday Night'. Don't knock it for we have all done it, even if we wished that the lens cap had still been on the camera.

On the move

Morris Minor, Austin A35, Ford Popular, Standard 8 and so many more makes and models of motor car, nearly all manufactured in this country, are a joy to behold for those of us who remember motoring before the invasion from the Far East changed the face of car parks and garage showrooms for good. We enjoyed straightforward names like Cowley, Cambridge, Oxford and Westminster for our models, unlike the pretentious Starlet, Carisma and Octavia we have been subjected to of late. The Plaza car park, with the cinema to the left and the Co-op to the right, was also used for rallies and time trials as cars churned up the dust on its clinker track. South Street is beyond the buildings, a shopping area that had, by this time, overtaken High Street as Romford's premier retail spot. Some said that it rivalled London's Oxford Street in style and chic. The cars were just as likely to have belonged to shoppers as to those watching the latest movie. The cinema was set back from the shops with a long, covered way leading up to it. Present day Stewards Walk follows that same line. It takes its name from the old Stewards Manor on the east side of Hornchurch Lane, as South Street was once known. The lands ran from there across to Squirrels Heath.

For a moment the reader could be excused in thinking that the camera had strayed onto the set of TV's 'Heartbeat', the popular series screened in the 1990s and early 2000s. Set in the Yorkshire Dales in the mid 1960s it has enjoyed long popularity, despite a changing cast of characters. The period setting is right, but it is not PC Rowan astride this motorbike, nor is it fat Alf standing alongside him. The policemen were overseeing part of Romford Carnival, though their body language suggested they would be glad when the day was over and they could retire to the police station for a well earned cuppa. The carnival was an enjoyable spectacle, but the children were something else. The scamps who took part in the decorated bicycle section enjoyed nothing better than teasing the local bobby. One little chap to the right even seems to be thumbing his nose at the boys in blue, though he would probably argue that it was just an itch. The older lads asked the motor cyclist why he had not joined in the spirit of the occasion and put some flowers on his machine. However, they did not labour the joke as it was still an era when a quick clip round the ear from an arm of the law brought parental approval rather than court action.

At first sight this might appear to be yet another wartime scene created by aerial bombardment we suffered in the blitz, but this fire occurred in the 1950s, though the devastation was just as final as that caused by any Junkers or Heinkel. The Dinette furniture factory, built on the site of the old goods yard, just outside Romford station on the line towards Gidea Park station, was one of the newer industries that had flourished in the town as we rebuilt our homes after the war, dispensing with the old, cumbersome styles of the 1930s and investing in the new, fashionable lines of the 1950s. Built close to rail connections with the rest of the country, the factory copied the practice of industries that had burgeoned a century before by ensuring easy access to modern transport. Eastern Counties Railways connected the line to the main line from London in 1839, providing Romford with an earlier rail link to the outside world than most other small towns of comparable size. The London, Tilbury and Southend line was later extended here and, as the London, Midland and Scottish (LMS) railway, built a station in South Street, opposite to, but linked with, Romford station's Great Eastern Railway, later the London and North Eastern Railway. Amalgamation took place in 1934 and the LMS station was converted into shops.

Below: This accident took place just outside Romford station, as can be seen from the electric pantograph that provides the power. No one was injured in the crash, but at least it made a change from disruption caused by leaves on the line or the wrong sort of snow that became standard and ludicrous excuses in more modern times. The car dealers waiting at the showroom for these models to grace their forecourts would have to wait to earn their commission. In the meantime, stocking up a little bit of body filler might have been a good idea. In the 21st century we have come to experience greater problems with ageing rolling stock and low investment, culminating in a rail service that has lost the confidence of many of its users. Lengthy delays and a series of horrific crashes have made people wary of committing themselves to a form of transport that once was the envy of the world. Restructuring has been in place for as long as most of us can remember. In the 1930s we were proud of the Cheltenham Flyer, Royal Scotsman, Silver Jubilee and

Coronation Scot trains that consistently set new, faster record times, leading to the Mallard's mind boggling 128 mph in 1938. After the war, nationalisation saw the beginning of a new era. By the 1960s we entered a new one as Dr Beeching axed many smaller stations and lines and the downward spiral began.

Bottom right: Remodelling of the roads, new barriers and one way systems around the town centre c1971

caused great confusion, as can be seen when this bus driver could not make up his mind whether to go left or right past the railings. Instead he opted for the middle course. The road sign indicates the way to the hospital and the railway station, a somewhat ironic touch as there might have been need of both following this accident. One would have provided treatment and the other an alternative means of getting home as this bus was going no further. Anyone wishing to hire the vehicle or one similar could ring the number advertised on the destination banner, but it was hardly a good advert for entrusting life and limb to the hands of those responsible for creating this lump of twisted metal. Puzzled bus company employees and crash investigators carefully examined the wreckage to try to determine the reason for the crash. In the meantime one passenger remained seated, steadfastly waiting to be allowed to complete his journey. He had tendered his exact fare as demanded and had no intention of budging until the service he had paid for had been completed in full. He was in for a long wait. Perhaps he had been annoyed by those dictatorial demands to proffer the correct fare to the bus driver. What a cheek! Why should the paying passenger have to do as he is told for surely it was up to the bus company to provide a service that included giving change? What happened to the maxim that the customer is always right?

Shopping spree

This is the face of Romford that anyone under the age of 40 will have difficulty in remembering and anyone yet to achieve 30 will never have experienced. The banks of market stalls are still with us, but they have been squashed a little further along Market Place towards High Street and St Edward's Church. Today the photographer would have to stand in the roundabout that links Main Road with the ring road of St Edward's Way and Mercury Gardens, risking life and limb if he ignored the underpass and tried to cross the road at ground level as thousands of vehicles per hour threaten his existence. It was so different in 1958 as just a handful of vehicles made their way along Market Place, heading past the shopping hall on the right. The scooters heading northeast became more than just a mode of travel in the 1960s. They became a fashion and cultural statement, owned by a section of youthful society known as the mods. They favoured the East Ham music of the Small Faces and allowed their hair to flow in the breeze, much to the annoyance of rockers on motorbikes whose world was one of grease and Gene Vincent. These gangs made their way to Southend and Clacton every Bank Holiday, hell bent on doing the other damage. Laurie Hall was a popular meeting place, though usually for more civilised groups than mods and rockers. It was completed in 1853 over the old Loam Pond and originally intended to be a courthouse, part of a scheme to improve this end of Romford.

Over 40 years ago the market throbbed with activity as people came from the small towns and villages around in search of bargains or merely to do their weekly shop. Although a bobby had been allocated point duty to help with the traffic flow, the roads were much quieter than anything we experience today. In the distance, on the far edge of Market Place, Laurie Hall stood as a monument to the London saddler who helped shape the face of that part of Victorian Romford. John Laurie, a man of Scottish ancestry, came to live at Marshalls in 1846. Around 1850 he helped to build the small middle class suburb of Laurie town that originally included both this hall and St Edward's Hall, erected on either side of the Loam pond in St Edward's Square, later to be called Laurie Square. Some other houses were built in the late 1850s on Park End Road. Laurie died in 1864 and St Edward's Hall did not long survive him. Laurie Hall lasted until 1970 when the vandals who masqueraded as men of vision decided that highways won more votes than edifices created a whole new vista for the area. Perhaps the reader can pause for a moment and ask a personal question. 'Would I prefer to look upon this scene or the one that greets my eyes today?'

Above: Romford had been granted the right to hold its originally weekly market over 700 years before this scene of c1960 was captured. The town was more than six miles from any other major settlement, the distance considered in medieval times to be the equivalent of a single day's sheep drive. Distances then were related to rural and creature considerations rather than the miles per gallon of fuel that is used as a modern basis of calculation. At first the market was held on a Wednesday, chiefly as an outlet for the leather trade in Hornchurch. Trade was probably at its peak in the 19th century, before the railways opened up greater vistas for the Victorian public. The annual Whit fair lasted from its inauguration in 1250 until 1877. After World War I, when a population boom began as many service personnel billeted here in 1914-18 decided to make Romford their peacetime home, attempts were made to hold a daily market. This only lasted for a few years, reverting to three per week in 1925. On the left, next to the Midland Bank, SW Adams' builders merchants, established on Market Place in 1900, was kept very busy in the first two decades after the second world war, helping provide materials for the growth in housing necessitated by rebuilding war damaged property and providing new homes for a population that grew from 88,000 in 1951 to 115,000 ten years later.

Romford Carnival brought the town to a standstill as gaily decorated floats, dancing troupes and marching bands paraded along Market Place on their way to Main Road and Raphael Park. The carnival raised a lot of money for local charity, as well as providing a fun day out for all the family. When Market Place was closed off to through traffic there was just nowhere for the carnival procession to go and a delightful focal point for local inhabitants and another lovely piece of tradition disappeared from this popular spot. The Liberty shopping complex now overlooks the market instead of the King's Head and its Charrington Ales. Other pubs that lost their identity included the old Windmill and Bells, though the float on the left was dedicated to tulip growing in Holland rather than any fond reminiscence for hand drawn beer. How things have changed on Market Place. Not only has the carnival passed by, but there will never again be the scenes that older readers can recall when cattle drovers brought their beasts to the pens in front of Stones, later Debenhams, to have them auctioned. The market was once the main cattle sales centre in South Essex, with large animal vans parked up on the side of the road as late as 1958.

The cyclist pedalling past Lloyd's Bank is coming from North Street towards South Street at the junction with Market Place to the left and High Street, part of the old London Road, to the right. In the 1960s this was a busy spot with pedestrians vying with other road users for right of way. The battle has now been won in favour of those on foot because so much of this part of town has been handed over to shoppers who can freely walk the streets without fear of being bowled over by vans, buses and cars that clogged the way and made us all wish that we had eyes in the backs of our heads as we tried to cross to the other pavement. Just next to the Quadrant Arcade, above British Home Stores, the first floor was home to a dance hall. There many couples had been able to enjoy the delights of ballroom dancing, showing off their talents with spin turns, neat chassis steps and fishtail footwork as they demonstrated their prowess in the waltz, foxtrot and quickstep. More exotic movements were mastered in the Latin dances of the samba, cha cha and pasodoble. But the 60s brought a dancing revolution that made dance halls old hat for the younger genera-tion. Small clubs sprang up with limited dancing space, necessi-tating new dances to evolve that needed less room and so the twist and the shake were born.

Stack 'em high is the message of the cut price supermarkets, but it seemed to have been adopted for a while by the planners who designed the concourse area from where shoppers can gain access to Market Place and The Liberty. Nicknamed 'the totem pole', the central feature typified architects' obsession in the 60s and 70s with rectangular shapes, whether they be huge office blocks or simple, decorative pieces. This structure was part of a complex of fountains that saw the water magically rise above the pools below before cascading down once more. The presence of so much flowing water had obviously affected a number of shoppers as they felt the need to form a queue for the toilets to the left! The water feature unfortunately attracted the attention of naughty children who took a delight in emptying washing up liquid into the pools. They were then able to enjoy the sight of bubbles rushing uphill before tumbling down in a foaming torrent. The whole structure was later removed and the space it vacated is used for different temporary stands and displays. Buskers sometimes entertain the crowds from near here, usually providing a harmless and enjoyable backdrop to the hustle and bustle of the stores beyond them.

Making a living

This is the life of our heritage as horses pulled the threshers and cutters in the cornfields around Eastern Avenue and farm labourers stacked high the sheaves that were symbolic of the heart of rural England. The inspiration for such works as HE Bates' 'My Uncle Silas' and 'Darling Buds of May', such scenes are important parts of our past that seem so far removed from this hurly burly world of the 21st century. Yet it was only a few generations back down the line that corn was brought to market and animals grazed in the meadows just outside Romford, waiting to be herded in small groups by drovers via the toll gates and on along the market plain. Little lads ran in front of the cattle, shutting householders' gates to prevent strays wandering into gardens and earning themselves a few coppers from grateful residents. Anyone foolish enough not to reward these urchins found that closed gates had been miraculously opened the next time that the herd lumbered past, leaving a nice display of decapitated daffodils and tulips in their wake. Livestock continued to be marshalled along Market Place to the cattle and sheep pens as late as the mid 1950s, but the only animals there these days are the dogs belonging to beggars trying to loosen heart and purse strings.

Above: There was a time when you could be both Jack of all trades and master of them as well. Emerson Park Halt, on the line to Southend, had just such a person in its stationmaster. Here was a man with a sense of pride in his work. Despite being someone fully qualified in his position he saw nothing strange in taking on other roles for he saw them part and parcel of the job. Imagine that today, with demarcation of tasks, job descriptions and lists of duties that would mean employing half a dozen people to take on his functions. Having sorted out the lighting he popped inside the little booking office to sell the tickets to any destination in the country to which a traveller wished to go, nipping out again shortly afterwards to collect those proffered by passengers alighting from the train. He kept the platform neat and tidy, as well as offering to lend a hand to any old lady struggling with her cases. He probably even used the little coal shovel propped against the wall to keep the station fires alight. The use of gas lighting seems incongruous as electrification of parts of the rail network in the London area had been around for two decades.

The fire at the Dinette furniture factory had firemen rushing for safety as the staircase collapsed and brickwork crashed to the ground around them. Amazingly, no one lost his life in the blaze, though several injuries were recorded. It is with such pictures that we can start to appreciate the dangers that the brave personnel of the emergency services take on our behalf. They are in there where it counts, putting their own safety second in their determination to help others. When this dramatic 1950s photograph was taken the firefighters were still not sure that no one was left trapped inside. The dedication of such crews was graphically illustrated by the sacrifices made in New York on 11 September 2001 when so many lost their lives rushing into the World Trade Centre to help those trapped in the terrorist attack that killed nearly 3,000. They could have stood back, but their sense of duty pushed them on to make the supreme sacrifice on behalf of others. In Romford a parish fire engine made its first appearance in 1787. By 1805 six firemen had been recruited and, in 1823, an engine house built on North Street in the garden of the workhouse. The fire service was still something of a hit and miss affair until Samuel Davis, a local builder, formed a volunteer brigade in 1890. As captain he recruited largely from his own workforce, building the fire station on Mawney Road that remained in use until 1960 when the new one opened in Pettits Lane North, close to the A12.

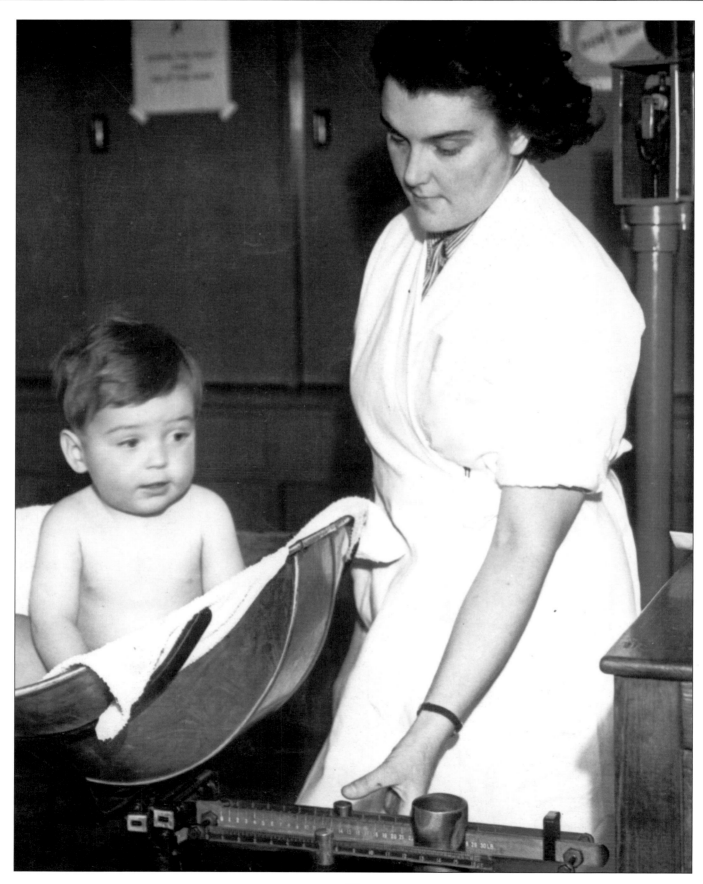

Both pages: It was possibly the acute wartime shortages of food and supplies which made doctors, health workers and mothers alike very aware of the health of the new generation, and children were carefully weighed, measured and immunised against the illnesses that had at one time meant disfigurement or even death (facing page). A vaccine for polio, the scourge of former years which left behind its terrible mark of wasted and useless limbs, only came later, however. American scientist Jonas Edward Salk developed a vaccine in 1955, and an oral vaccine was produced in 1960. The vaccines brought the dreaded disease under control and today polio is rarely seen. On a day to day basis, vitamins were vital to the health of children, and long before the advent of the cod liver oil capsule, the recommended spoonful of cod liver oil was administered to the youngest children every day in schools and nurseries around the country during the 1940s. Children might have screwed up their noses at the fishy taste, but the nourishing cod liver oil went a long way towards keeping them healthy. The vitamin-packed orange juice was far more palatable, and artful mothers would often use the orange juice as a bribe: no cod liver oil, no

orange juice. Following hard on the heels of the oil, the juice took away the distinctive taste that was disliked by so many children. Ante-natal clinics did all they could to check on the diet, blood pressure and vitamin intake of mothers to be; our carefully posed photograph, taken in an ante-natal clinic in the 1930s, records at least the cleanliness and tidiness that was to their great credit (bottom). And when the tiny new citizen finally arrived, there were health visitors to pay friendly calls on families in their homes to check on the health and happiness of mothers and babies (left). National Dried Milk for babies was also made available to mothers, and before today's push towards natural feeding NDM was for decades very much in vogue. We need to remember that at the time of these photographs the National Health service did not exist, and in fact the NHS only came into operation after World War II in July 1948.

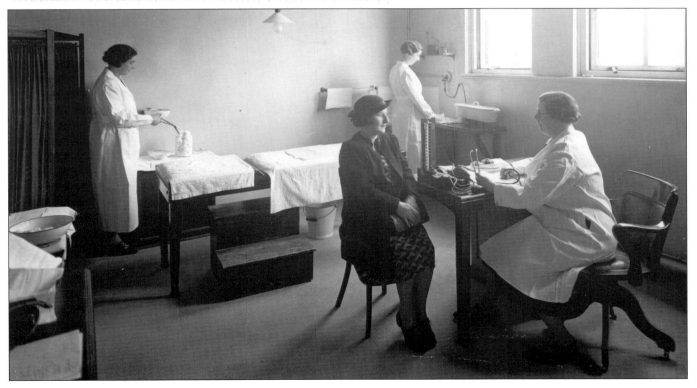

Laurie Hall was often used as a venue for meetings and rallies where informed opinion could be aired or debated in a rational manner. Not so when the Blackshirts came to town, for they whipped up a storm of racial and religious bigotry wherever they went. The result was nearly always the same, catcalling degenerating into violence with missile throwing and fisticuffs becoming the order of the day. The police held the middle ground, often bearing the brunt of the abuse from both sides. In the early 1960s John F Kennedy, president of the USA, had begun a programme of civil rights measures designed to improve the lot of those downtrodden people, especially blacks, for whom there seemed little justice in everyday life. The mood of greater tolerance was copied in Britain, but produced the inevitable backlash from extremist groups. Sir Oswald Mosley, surrounded by a bodyguard of thugs known as 'biff boys', appeared on his soapbox once more. In 1932 he had founded the British Union of Fascists, allying himself with much of the political, anti Semitic dogma of Hitler and Mussolini. He was interned for three years during the war, but continued to spew out his message of hate when forming the Union Movement in 1948. In 1962 it appeared just like old times when his attempts to address rallies in Trafalgar Square, the East End, Romford and other areas around the capital were broken up amid a barrage of coins, fruit and fists. Mosley, whose wife was Diana, one of the Mitford girls, died in 1980, aged 84, still convinced that the world was run by communists and Jews.

Uniform, oblong concrete, steel and glass structures were all that architects and planners could come up with in the 60s and 70s. They were easy to manufacture and erect, but did you not long for one tiny bit of individuality that would mark one building out from the rest? You could be anywhere in Britain when you looked at the new maternity wing at the hospital in Rush Green. A baby boom, though not as dramatic as the postwar one but significant enough, took place in the mid 1960s as couples enjoyed the increased prosperity of the era by deciding that they could afford to bring another mouth to feed into the world. An increase in the number of expectant mums, allied to the need to revamp some of the older hospital buildings, gave Romford the opportunity to provide this additional facility. Extra personnel were needed to staff the unit and some recruitment was made from overseas, as it had been in the 1950s when the country faced a shortage and turned to the Commonwealth countries to help us out. Let us hope that some of the babies they delivered became architectural designers and are now entering an era when they can influence the future shape of Britain's buildings. Is it too much to ask for the occasional buttress, the merest hint of a crenellation, a modest cornice or the odd cupola? Even one of those quaint Victorian gargoyles would break up the rigid lines.

Potting the lot

Snooker. It was a game invented by bored army officers stationed in India in the 19th century, as an alternative to the often rather boring billiards; and it soon made it back to Blighty to become one of the favourite pastimes of men of all classes. Being good at snooker however was, as we all know, a sign of a mis-spent youth.

But at least those of us who spent, or mis-spent, the spare hours of our youth in the smoke filled snooker halls above Burton's the Tailors enjoyed ourselves. We puffed manfully on our Woodbines and tried to emulate the likes of the legendary Joe Davis and make a name for ourselves in a sport we could all play - or thought we could.

How the game has moved on. It's hard to believe that we once listened to the commentary on snooker matches on the wireless; it's even harder to believe that

Above: *Barry Hearn, founder of Matchroom Sport.*
Below: *The early days at the Romford Snooker Centre.*

for a while snooker almost died out with billiard halls closing down all over the country and the only players in the few remaining clubs all seeming to be old men.

What happened to transform the game from one about to join the ranks of royal tennis and croquet as a game we know of but few take any interest in? The answer of course was television -and more importantly colour television. When the BBC's Pot Black programme began in a small way in the late 1960s who could have predicted the long term impact it would have? Maybe many of us still watched on black and white sets and had to puzzle out which of the grey balls was red, brown, yellow or green but we were still hooked. But not as hooked as we were going to be.

Pot Black introduced us to the world of the professional snooker player, that then small band of experts whom many had no idea even existed. Men who could actually

How has that change come about? In part the answer is promotion. And the greatest name in promotion is undoubtedly Barry Hearn and his Romford based company Matchroom Sport Ltd with its headquarters in Western Road.

Since starting up in 1982 the Matchroom name has meant being a winner - for both the sports personalities whom Matchroom represents and in the successful sports events with which it has been associated.

The driving force behind the Matchroom top team is Barry Hearn - a dynamic combination of trained accountant, entrepreneur and genuine sports fan. He saw the untapped potential of snooker and set about transforming the fortunes of its players. From that early vision Matchroom Snooker grew into the world's premier snooker promoter and leader in developing the game worldwide.

Barry Hearn qualified as a Chartered Accountant in 1970 and spent several years with a major firm of international accountants before moving into the commercial world as finance director of Kensal House Investments. After brief flirtations with both the fashion industry and property development he became chairman of Lucania Snooker Clubs in 1974 and began to involve the snooker hall chain in amateur tournament promotions.

make a modest living playing exhibition matches for money: men like gentlemanly Ray Reardon and the avuncular Fred Davis - and all those other mature men who had kept the flame alive and who suddenly found themselves playing for their professional lives against the young upstart, the Irish Hurricane, Alex Higgins who astonished us with his virtuosity with a cue.

When Alex Higgins won the World Snooker Championship the prize money was just £350. How the world changes; today the prizes available to professional snooker players are measured in hundreds of thousands of pounds and far from scraping a living the best amongst them enjoy millionaire lifestyles.

*Above: Barry Hearn, and friends outside the Romford Snooker Centre in the late 1970s. **Right:** The boxing match featuring Frank Bruno and Joe Bugner, promoted by Barry Hearn in 1987.*

In 1976 the young Steve Davis began playing at the Romford Lucania Club and he and Barry Hearn struck up a friendship and association which was to have a major influence on the world of snooker when Steve would turn out to be one of the greatest snooker players in the entire history of the sport. In 1982 Riley Leisure acquired the chain of Lucania Snooker Clubs for £3.1 million leaving Barry free to concentrate on the development of snooker both in the UK and overseas. With the support of the Matchroom professional players Barry promoted snooker all over the world and has been particularly instrumental in promoting the game in the Far East.

Barry began his involvement in big time boxing by diving straight in at the deep end and staging the Joe Bugner Vs Frank Bruno heavyweight show-down at Tottenham's White Hart Lane Stadium in 1987 in front of 30,000 people. From that auspicious beginning then the Matchroom Boxing stable would rise to the top in both Britain and Europe staging over 50 promotions throughout the season including British, Commonwealth, European and World Championship bouts.

Together with Eurosport, ITV and Sky, who would televise Matchroom shows, Barry helped to discover and develop such champions as Chris Eubank, Nigel Benn, Herbie Hide, Francis Ampofo, Steve Collins, Jim McDonnell, Michael Ayers and Steve Roberts and of course Prince Naseem Hamed.

Married to Susan and with two children, Barry lists his sporting interests as boxing, snooker, 9 ball pool, crick-

Top right: *Barry Hearn's first boxing show featured Gary Mason (centre) and was promoted with Terry Lawless (right).* **Top left:** *Alex Higgins and Steve Davis.* **Right:** *Cliff Thorburn.*

et, golf and more recently football. Whilst he has no pretensions about his snooker skills - or come to that his boxing ability - Barry is a fanatical golfer and has even been known to take a few racks off world-class pool players.

Whilst sports such as snooker and boxing had become firmly established as two of the most popular sports on television Barry Hearn set his considerable sights on other immensely popular but less well known sports. By 1994 Barry would be promoting the world's richest coarse fishing match - Fish'O'Mania - live on Sky Sports for six hours an event which was destined to become an annual fixture in the sporting calendar.

The Marlin World Cup from Mauritius would become yet another blue chip event in the Matchroom portfolio. Following on from promoting fishing Barry would become

with Barry would agree when he says something is going to happen... it will.

As we enter the new Millennium a range of other sporting activities have been added to Matchroom Sport's portfolio. Matchroom Golf, run by Barry's son Eddie, manages many golfers on the European Tour including Greg Owen, John Bickerton, Jonathan Lomas and David Lynn.

In 2001 Matchroom Sport acquired the Europro Golf Tour, which is televised and syndicated worldwide and the Tour Final took place at the Parque da Floresta on the Western Algarve, Portugal.

Tenpin Bowling has been another major addition to Matchroom Sport's events, with the AMF World Cup, The Weber Cup and the World Masters being staged each year.

Poker also looks to be a growth area for Matchroom Sport with the inaugural Poker Million being staged in London in March 2002, with a £1M prize to the winner and live coverage of the final events play shown to a massive UK audience on Sky TV!

It's a long way from snooker on the wireless!

Top left: *Snooker pro's team up for their annual golf day.* ***Above left:*** *Dennis Taylor signs up with Barry Hearn following his epic victory over Steve Davis in 1985.* ***Below:*** *Barry Hearn and colleagues on a promotional tour of China in the early 1980s.*

intent on developing the game of pool from a leisurely pub game into a huge TV sport; the success of Matchroom's Mosconi Cup, Europe v America match and the World 9 Ball Pool Masters would be a testament to the progress which could be made with Barry's backing. In the summer of 1999 Matchroom eventually promoted the inaugural World Professional Pool Championship - the biggest event in the history of the game.

In March 1995 Barry Hearn assumed a controlling interest in Leyton Orient Football Club. Barry had major plans for the club, including stadium development, a project which would commence in the Summer of 2000.

As Barry Hearn's Matchroom organisation has grown so have the bank balances of the sportsmen and women associated with it - and as anyone who has ever worked

New York, Paris ... and Romford

At Ashton Road, Harold Hill can be found the premises of Chauvin Pharmaceuticals Ltd. The history of the site and its changing ownership provides a fascinating example of how the world of business functions, and how events over the course of more than a century, and in many parts of the globe, can impact on one small corner of England.

The original building at the north end of the site adjacent to Faringdon Avenue and Ashton Road was built in the mid 1950s and was then leased by the London Hospital (Ligature Department) company which manufactured natural cat gut (which, incidentally, is short for cattle gut and nothing to do with cats) and synthetic sutures or 'stitches'. The area was acquired by Smith & Nephew Associated Companies in March 1971 for a price of £175,063 when the London Hospital (Ligature Department) Ltd went into liquidation.

Prior to the 1950s the site was open fields with ponds touching on three corners of the site, with Haroldwood Farm to the north and a collection of farm buildings known as the Warrens to the south.

Right: Pouching of multidose adrenaline eye drops. Below: Chauvin Pharmaceuticals Romford site prior to factory erection in the 1950s.

Thomas James Smith, a pharmacist born in Grantham in Lincolnshire, had started in business as a chemist in Hull in 1856 with £500 borrowed from his father; he soon diverted into the manufacture and supply of cod liver oil. In 1896 TJ Smith, by now suffering from ill health, formed a partnership with his nephew Horatio Smith leading to the birth of TJ Smith & Nephew cod-liver oil suppliers. TJ Smith died later that same year.

At the time of the founder's death the firm had a staff of just three and an annual turnover of £3,000, £2,500 of which was in sales of cod-liver oil. By 1912, under the leadership of the young Horatio Smith, the company had expanded to employ a staff of over fifty, many of whom were manufacturing rolled and cut bandages which were being sold to the Turkish War Office for Turkey's war in the Balkans. On the strength of that experience the company was able to accept an order from the French government in 1914, at the outset of the first world war, for field dressings worth £350,000. During the four years of the war the company would take over every building in Hull's Neptune Street its staff increasing from fifty to over 1200 and achieve a turnover of more than £2 million.

With the end of the Great War in 1918 and the end of demand for bandages and dressings the staff shrank to just 183 but were saved from further redundancies by the Factory Act of 1924 which required all employers to have first aid kits on their premises. Other developments soon followed: marketing the newly invented Elastoplast from 1928 for example, and in 1930 the company's famous plaster of Paris bandage 'Gypsona'.

*Top: Smith & Nephew Pharmaceuticals Romford site in the late 1970s. **Above centre:** Adrenaline eye drops manufacturing plant.*

In 1937 Smith & Nephew became a public company - Smith & Nephew Associated Companies Ltd. The company was now a group and its original capital had grown to £500,000.

The TJ Smith group of companies, widely known as SANACO, was involved in the manufacture of a huge range of products in toiletries, plastics, textiles, clothing, as well as the medical and pharmaceutical fields. By 1949 the company could afford to spend a million pounds building a new factory in Hull to meet the demand for sales.

For many years SANACO were world leaders in the treatment of tuberculosis and largely due to its efforts in making available the necessary drugs for its treatment the incidence of TB declined sharply during the 1940s and 50s.

Looking to expand the range of its products the company moved into ophthalmic products with the firm eventually becoming one of the most important to produce products for the treatment of glaucoma, a range of solutions for diagnostic purposes and of contact lens solutions.

Further important products which would also be marketed world wide would be a sterile cream for the treatment of burns along with products such as sedatives and pain killers.

In September 1960 'nephew' Horatio Smith died at the age of 82 ending the link between the company and its founders; the company would shortly own 40 companies in the United Kingdom and 30 overseas.

TJ Smith & Nephew had transferred the manufacture of 'Minims' unit dose eye drops and contacts lens solutions from its site in Hull to the newly acquired Romford site in 1971 and also had a component warehouse based in Tonbridge Road on Harold Hill industrial estate. The new site was incorporated into Smith & Nephew Pharmaceuticals Ltd, a subsidiary which had been established in 1957. Finished product was transferred to Smith & Nephew's central distribution warehouse in Bessemer Road, Welwyn Garden City.

Later on Smith & Nephew Optics Ltd joined the site and manufactured Hydron hard and soft contact lenses and this was subsequently incorporated into Smith & Nephew Chiromed based at Walthamstow in 1982.

In June 1982 Smith & Nephew Pharmaceuticals acquired the site adjacent to Faringdon Avenue in Ashton Road for £250,000. The site was leased from the London County Council to Kinlochs (a division of Booker McDonnell plc) a provisions merchant who cured bacon on the site.

In 1983 the area vacated by Smith & Nephew Optics was developed into a new sterile suite for the manufacture of Flamazine an anti-bacterial cream used in the treatment of third degree burns.

That same year Smith & Nephew Pharmaceuticals relocated its sales, marketing, regulatory affairs and distribution from Bessemer Road in Welwyn Garden City, to a newly leased site in Bampton Road some two hundred yards from the manufacturing site.

Ten years later however, in 1993 Smith & Nephew plc decided to concentrate on its core business activity of 'healthcare' and so looked to find a buyer for Smith & Nephew Pharmaceuticals.

In December 1993 Groupe Chauvin a French pharmaceutical company acquired the ophthalmic division of Smith & Nephew Pharmaceuticals based at Romford as well as the recently privatised East German ophthalmic pharmaceutical manufacturer Ankerpharm. The non ophthalmic products manufactured at Romford were incorporated into a new company Smith & Nephew Healthcare based in Hull.

The new arrival in Romford, Groupe Chauvin, was privately owned by a French ophthalmologist Dr Bernard Chauvin, the company having been founded by his grandfather Alfred Chauvin in the 1880s and whose 'Laboratoire Chauvin' would develop some 10,000 formulae during the founder's lifetime.

Top: *Posters advertising some of the products manufactured in Romford.* **Left:** *A Flamazine Cream manufacturing vessel.*

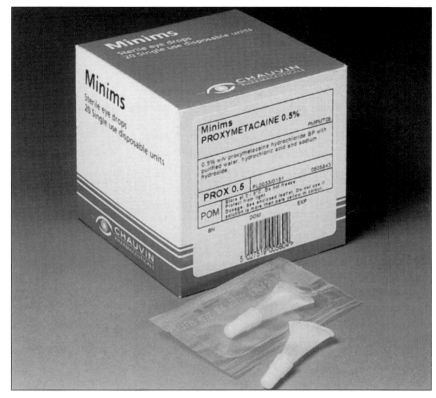

all ophthalmic manufacture currently undertaken by Chauvin Pharmaceuticals in England would be transferred to Laboratoire Chauvin in Aubenas in France.

At the end of 1997 the finished goods distribution warehouse in Hillman Close Hornchurch was closed and the operations incorporated into the Ashton Road site at Romford.

In August 2000 Bausch & Lomb, the America-based world's number one eye care company with headquarters in Rochester, New York State, acquired Groupe Chauvin as part of its strategy to create a European pharmaceutical division. Between November 2000 and July 2001 Bausch & Lomb integrated Chauvin Pharmaceuticals sales and marketing functions in the UK at its headquarters at Kingston upon Thames leaving the Romford site as a stand alone manufacturing unit in its European supply chain.

Not long after coming to Romford the Chauvin group could boast ownership of no fewer than seven companies in Europe with established markets for its prescription drugs in ophthalmology, ocular surgery and family medication in France, the UK, Germany, Switzerland, Benelux and Portugal and exports to more than 120 countries.

Chauvin Pharmaceuticals, now a division of Bausch & Lomb, continues to manufacture Minims, the world's largest range of preservative free sterile eye drops. With an ever growing global demand, over 32 million Minims units were produced in 2000 at Romford.

Smith & Nephew Pharmaceuticals Ltd continued to operate out of the Bampton Road site throughout 1994 and therefore Chauvin Pharmaceuticals relocated its distribution warehouse to a unit in Hillman Close in Hornchurch.

Above left: *Minims carton and individual Minims units, the company's main product.* ***Below:*** *Chauvin Pharmaceuticals, moving into the 21st Century.*

Throughout 1994 and 1995 Smith & Nephew built a new sterile manufacturing facility for the production of Flamazine cream at its site in Hull and the last batch of Flamazine was manufactured at Romford in March 1996.

In June 1996 Groupe Chauvin announced that

A *winning formula*

How we enjoy racing of every kind. We are all fascinated with speed and sporting prowess. Almost the first thing man did after domesticating the dog was to race one dog against that of a neighbour. And more than likely they enjoyed a small wager on the outcome.

Thousands of years later the setting may no longer be an open glade, and we may not have to sit on a rock to watch, but the sense of fun and excitement watching superb dogs race against one another has not changed in the least.

Romford began greyhound racing on 21st June 1929, the track moved to its present site two years later. Many changes have been made since those first race meetings, and no doubt many more are still to come. The Coral company purchased the London Road track in 1976 - and Coral's present owners, Morgan Grenfell Private Equity, took the helm in 1999.

In the early 1920s Romford-born Lieutenant Colonel Archer Frederick Leggett OBE would hold greyhound races in a field behind his house. In 1929 he found a better site in London Road, beside the Crown Inn, opposite the site of the present stadium.

Two years later, when the landlord of the Crown, who owned the site, asked for more rent, Archer Leggett and his associate Michael Pohl decided to move across the road to the present site.

To begin with five meetings a week were held, on Tuesdays, Thursdays and Saturdays plus two meetings on Sunday. Admission prices were 1s 6d for men and half price - just 9d - for ladies.

Things were not quite as well organised then as they would be in later decades. The antics of the hare were as entertaining as anything else; the hare reportedly dashed all over and across the track colliding with the stanchions and the wire placed to protect the spectators. Those who

Above: Early greyhound transportation, circa 1950.
Below: Collecting money for the war effort.
Below left: Keeping an eye on the competition!

competing; in the post war years it faced competition from stadia at Southend, Rayleigh and Dagenham. But none could match the atmosphere at Romford - or Romford's greyhounds. On May 1st 1951 Romford Stadium won the Dagenham and Reading News of the World National Inter-Track competition, the winner of the race receiving £12 and a replica of the trophy to take home.

Archer Leggett had been born in 1900, upon the arrival of Coral he was aged 76 and retired from the stadium's Management Committee to become Life President.

attended all had a great time.

However not everyone approved. In 1930 the Romford Urban Council unanimously voted against greyhound tracks, trotting tracks and speedway. The Council proposed that the new greyhound track should be closed without compensation for the owners.

As history records however, to the great relief of generations of Romford race goers, the move failed.

And how customers flocked to the races, not least when in 1937 Archer Leggett caused a considerable sensation by introducing African cheetah racing to Romford as an unusual change from greyhounds!

Nor was racing the only sport on offer. That same year the London Amateur League won the championship Cup for American Baseball. And as well as baseball the stadium also hosted its share of boxing matches too.

On 22nd October 1950 disaster struck Romford Stadium when a fire broke out in the Popular Enclosure causing significant damage. Fortunately the damage was regarded as no more than a temporary inconvenience and the enclosure was soon rebuilt. Romford was not the only local Greyhound stadium

Over the years Archer Leggett had seen many changes to the stadium, yet one of the biggest was still to come: the opening of a 240 seat restaurant. A hundred new air conditioned kennels were installed in 1996 and the whole racing circuit was redesigned in 1997. The refurbished Millennium Stand was officially opened in July 1999 with a new children's play area completed for the start of the millennium. It came as no surprise when in its 70th anniversary in 1999 Romford Greyhound Stadium was formally declared Racecourse of the Year by the industry.

Today Romford Greyhound Stadium is looking forward to the future with even more plans for further investment to ensure that it remains the best greyhound track in Britain.

*Top left: Under starters orders. **Above left:** Another happy winner. **Below:** The new children's play area behind the Millennium Stand within the Millennium Enclosure.*

Precision progress

The years following the end of the second world war presented massive opportunities for those with the will to start their own businesses. Thousands of small firms were started up as post-war prosperity fuelled economic optimism. The best of them grew slowly and steadily, quietly establishing solid reputations as a result of hard work and attention to the quality of their products and service to their customers.

One such was the A.R.G.E.E. Instrument Co Ltd founded in 1951 by Raymond Humphrey Goss; the firm taking its name from his initials; he could not have suspected that more than fifty years later the firm would still be going strong.

Raymond Goss had moved to Hornchurch as a young child where he showed a strong tendency towards a career in engineering, practising at home by dismantling household appliances - and amazingly being able to reassemble them in perfect working order.

With his obvious talent young Raymond went to study engineering at Leyton Technical College where he became a successful student before leaving to start an apprenticeship at Woolwich Arsenal in 1939. The Monday he began work was the day after the second world war was declared: his mother packed him off that morning with his gas mask fearing she would never see him again.

Raymond however survived unscathed and left Woolwich Arsenal at the end of the war to set up his own business in Leytonstone. The venture was short-lived however as he was soon called up for National Service. After two years in the Forces, in 1951, he tried again and this time started a new business in Romford operating from 14 Albert Road, the same premises which are still in use. On that firm foundation was begun the business which is still flourishing today.

The new firm began producing photographic equipment such as enlargers and supplementing that business by taking on general engineering work.

The youthful Raymond was full of energy and enterprise, working very long hours to get his business off the ground. So energetic, however, was Raymond that very soon after the start of his business he even began another major project, having a house built to his own design in Nelmes Way, the house which would eventually become the Goss family home.

In 1957, at the age of 34, Raymond met his future wife Pamela and married two years later. Seven years after getting married however Raymond developed multiple sclerosis, a disease which sadly disabled him for the remainder of his life; he had always been an active man and struggled to come to terms with his illness. Despite his difficulties he managed, with great courage and determination, to overcome his physical problems and keep the business thriving and continuing, despite the odds, to provide for himself, his wife, their young son, and of course his loyal workforce.

Above: *Company founder Raymond Goss.*

The photography equipment side of the business lasted for some 15 or so years until the engineering side of the business outgrew it. The business had always leaned towards the specialist precision and small component manufacturer for clients such as the MOD and the aerospace and communications industries. That has grown and continues with other high tech industries such as medical equipment manufacturers now joining the customer base of mostly blue chip companies spread all across the UK and which require relatively small quantities of very high precision work.

Today's managing director is Raymond and Pamela's son, Nigel, who started working with his father in 1988. In the future the firm intends to explore other potential markets to further expand the already large customer base, and with this in mind is currently investing in the latest measuring and computer technology to keep the business at the very top of the market in order to continue to enjoy a steady, sustained growth.

Marking the firm's 50th anniversary in 2001 the present owners and its many long serving members of staff could look back with understandable satis-

faction. They could reflect not only on 50 years of excellence but also look back at the history of an extremely stable company with an equally stable workforce whose future, thanks to the firm foundations laid by Raymond Goss, looks as secure as its past.

Above: *Precision engineering in the early days.*
Below: *The current workforce at the start of a new millennium.*

Carnival time in the 1960s.

Acknowledgments

The publishers would like to thank

Roy Squire

Andrew Mitchell

Steve Ainsworth